Christmas WRAPPINGS

Basics and Ideas for Perfectly Wrapped Gifts

By Philippa Kirby

Wrappings Designed by Alison Lee
with Lois Steinhardt

A TERN BOOK

Copyright © 1986 by Tern Enterprises, Inc.

All rights reserved. No reproduction of this book in whole or in part or in any form may be made without written authorization of the copyright owner. Published by Weidenfeld & Nicolson, New York, a division of Wheatland Corporation.

ISBN 1-55584-009-4

Library of Congress Cataloguing in Publication Data

Kirby, Philippa, 1960–
  Christmas wrappings.

  1. Gift wrappings.   2. Christmas.   I. Title.
TT870.K534   1986   745.54   86-5617

CHRISTMAS WRAPPINGS:
Basics and Ideas for Perfectly Wrapped Gifts
was prepared and produced by
Tern Enterprises, Inc.
Sagaponack Road
Bridgehampton, New York 11932

Editor: Karla Olson
Art Director: Mary Moriarty
Designer: Alison Lee
Photo Research: Susan M. Duane
Production Manager: Karen L. Greenberg
Photography: Tony Cenicola

Typeset by Paragraphics
Color separations by Hong Kong Scanner Craft Company Ltd.
Printed and bound in Hong Kong by Leefung-Asco Printers Ltd.

Contents

My thanks to Karla Olson for being so careful and intelligent; to Alison Lee for her ideas and her attention to detail; to Louise Quayle for bringing it up in the first place; to Val Clarke and Michael Collins for help, interest, and encouragement; and to John and Maryette, without whom I would not be around to do the book at all.

Beginning With the Basics

All you need for a well-done, creative wrapping is a few basics and a handful of supplies. To begin, have on hand a pair of large, sharp scissors and lots of disappearing tape. Start by wrapping something with a uniform shape, such as a cardboard shirt box. Decide how much paper you need by placing the box on the paper you have chosen and loosely covering the box with it as if you were going to wrap it. The paper should cover three of the box's sides once and one of the narrow sides twice. Cut the paper and lay it, right side down, on a flat surface. Place the box on the paper, with side D close to one of the short ends (see illustration page 7). Make a short fold in the other short end so that about an inch (two-

and-a-half centimeters) of the right side of the paper shows. Wrap the paper all the way around the box until the edge with the fold runs exactly along the edge that joins sides B and D. Adjust the paper slightly if the folded edge is not quite flush with the B edge. Spend a couple of seconds to make the seam a perfect, invisible match. A mismatched seam or a seam in the middle of one of the sides of your package ruins the clean look.

Do not be skimpy with the tape when you secure your main seam. If you use several tiny pieces, the paper may gap between pieces or tear at the tape edges. Ideally, run the tape the length of the seam. This will also make the next folds easier.

Trim the paper on the unfolded edges. Too much paper will make your package ends bulky, and you will have to wrestle with the paper to get it to do what you want. A little more than the width of side C or E is the ideal length. On one end, fold the top down so that you have two paper triangles sticking out on the sides, with sharply creased edges. Fold the triangles in toward the box. The still-extending paper will have sloping sides and a long, raw edge. Carefully fold up a small lip on the long edge, then bring this folded edge all the way up to meet the top of the box. The seam should run along the box edge. If you find you have an overlap, go back and adjust the lip you folded. Again, be generous with the tape. Repeat the folds on the other end.

BASIC WRAP

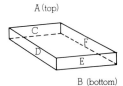

BOTTLE WRAP

CANDY WRAP

Christmas Wrappings

Once you have mastered wrapping a box, you will find it easy to manipulate the paper to tackle oddly shaped presents. If you use a paper without an obvious "right" and "wrong" side, anything goes. Crumple and twist tissue paper into any shape you want.

Roll a wine bottle up in a large sheet of brightly colored tissue paper so that you have a cylinder, with the paper extending about two inches (five centimeters) out from the bottle base and about six inches (twenty-one centimeters) above the bottle top. Fold the long, exposed edge that runs up the bottle under and tape the main seam as you did with the box. Make four evenly spaced cuts in the base end of the paper, all the way to the bottom of the bottle, and fold the sides in so that the paper overlaps and the bottle has a squared bottom. Discreetly tape the ends down. Twist the paper in around the bottle neck and tape as sparingly and unobtrusively as possible. Twist the paper above the top of the bottle neck. Make vertical cuts in the excess paper, and fluff out the ends.

Use the candy wrapper approach with a soft toy or anything else pliable. Roll the gift in the middle of a piece of supple paper so that the gift is completely covered and an ample amount of paper extends from each end. Fold a small edge of the long seam over, then secure it with tape from each end of the gift. Gather the paper at the top and bottom of the gift and secure with tape (which you can then hide with ribbon). Cut and fluff the ends.

The perfect complement and finishing touch to almost any wrap is ribbon. Use ribbon to elaborate on a theme already created with your paper, or as a contrast. A beautiful bow adds the crowning touch to any gift—and it is simple to make your own.

The easiest and most versatile ribbon to work with is ribbed curling ribbon. Without cutting the ribbon, estimate how much you will need by wrapping the ribbon loosely around the package. The amount of excess you will need depends on the kind of bow you decide to use. For a simple knot, add about four inches (ten centimeters) of ribbon; for a simple bow, add about eight inches (twenty centimeters). In any case, be generous. You can snip off excess ribbon, but you are stuck if the ribbon too short. For a basic but lovely embellishment, cut the ribbon as if for a simple knot, and put it on a flat surface. Lay the wrapped box in the center of the ribbon, on either side A or B. Bring the ribbon up and carefully twist it forty-five degrees so that the twist lies flat against the box. Turn the box over and bring the ribbon around, then

ARCING BOW

TWIST BOW

PROTECTIVE BOX

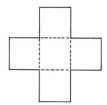 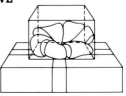

secure it at the center of the package with a double knot, not a bow. Tie about six even lengths of ribbon around your first knot, so you have fourteen pieces of ribbon, all with the same center. Do not worry if the ribbon ends are not evenly spaced; it is the nature of ribbon to fall nonsymmetrically. Pull each tendril hard against the blade of a pair of scissors so they curl. You will now have a mass of ringlets. This look adds extravagance and fullness. Try curling ribbon around the neck of a wrapped wine bottle; tendrils of different lengths will tumble down the front of the bottle like bubbling champagne.

A deceptively simple arcing bow adds a sleek touch to a high-tech wrap. First, instead of tying the ribbon around the package, create two loops held together on the bottom with tape. (The effect is smoother than the usual twist.)

Then cut five lengths of the same ribbon in decreasing size—nine and a half inches, eight inches, six and a half inches, four inches, and two and a half inches (twenty-four centimeters, twenty centimeters, sixteen centimeters, ten centimeters, and six centimeters) are good lengths, though any combination of ribbon lengths in an even ratio works well. You can also add longer or shorter ribbons at either end of the scale. Make each length into a loop securing the ends both inside and outside with a small piece of tape. Place the largest loop on a flat surface and press the middle of the loop down. Put the second largest loop on top of the first and press the middle down. Repeat this until you come to the smallest loop. Using a thumbtack or a pin, make a small hole in the center of your bow to hold the loops together temporarily. Either staple the loops together at this point or, if the bow is thick, make a small stitch with a needle and thread.

This bow also serves as the basis for a full rosette bow. Instead of cutting just one piece of ribbon for each length, cut three or four to make a very full bow. Use the same principle as with the arcing bow, but spread the loops of the same length in several directions.

There is another, even simpler twist bow that looks full and rich. Wrap a generous length of flat ribbon about fifteen times around the four fingers of your left hand. Secure with a small piece of tape at the end. Push the sides of the ribbon loop together until the loop is flat. Hold it while you trim away small triangles from both sides of the ribbons at each end. Be sure to cut through all layers of ribbon, but do not cut the triangles so that the points overlap and break the loop. Now, press the top portion of the ribbon circle down

so the two diamonds meet. Secure
them with a small piece of ribbon
twisted, then tied around the center.
Pull the loops out, one layer at a time,
with a twisting action. You now have
thirty loops, emanating in all directions.
Twist the loops carefully when you pull
them out to give the bow its distinctive
fullness.

Bows made independently of the ribbon around a package are most easily
attached with small arcing lengths of
the same ribbon. Slip the ribbon
through one of the bottom loops of the
bow or around the center of the full
bow. Tie a small knot and trim the ends
very close to the knot. Another easy
way to attach a bow is to make a small
loop of tape, with the sticky side out.
Attach the loop to the bottom of the
bow and then to the package.

Once you have mastered the basic
wrapping and bow-tying techniques,

you have a package that can be mailed. The more uncluttered a wrapping, the better the chance that it will arrive at its destination the way it left you. Small gifts can be sent in book envelopes, but decorate the outside enticingly. Paint a big ribbon across the envelope, add stickers, draw musical notes with carol words written underneath them, and write the recipient's name in calligraphy. If you want to pack the present in a box, you can come up with fun variations on packing materials: air-popped popcorn, packing straw held round the gift with a bright ribbon or in layers separated by different colors of tissue paper, and Sunday comics balled up.

If you want to mail a gift with a bow, construct a protective cube and put it gently over the bow. Take a piece of cardboard that is a little larger than three times the size of your bow. Cut it as in the diagram on page 11. With a razor blade, make slits in the board at the dotted lines, being careful not to cut all the way through the board. Fold down along the dotted lines, then place a small piece of tape over each forty-five-degree angle to secure it. Set the box over the bow. You can hold it in place with a small piece of tape but the paper may tear when the box is removed. Hold the box in place by stuffing packing material around it; then there will be no danger of ruining your wrapping.

The only limitation to your wrappings is your imagination. Go to variety stores and let the toys and trinkets available there suggest ideas. Take a notepad with you and write down ideas as they occur to you. As you buy presents, stop and consider how you want to wrap each gift, then pick up the supplies you need. This will save you a last-minute scramble on Christmas Eve.

Designs by Theme

Wrapping a gift and putting a bow on it is not the whole story. The look you create with paper and ribbon should be carefully tailored to suit the recipient. A wrap for a colleague is

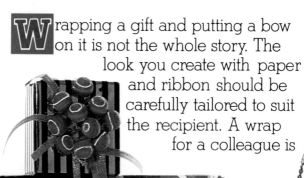

probably very different from one for your sister. You want the wrapping for your colleague to be polished and attractive, but you want your sister to see something familiar in a wrap.

Start by asking: Is there a particular style that will enhance the gift? A compact disc player will look great in a wrap that is sleek and hi-tech. Nestle a mohair sweater in a romantic package that is textured and alluring. Is a country look closer to what your present wants? Or is your gift whimsical and fun so that it calls for a package

that brings back childhood Christmases, Santa, and Frosty the Snowman?

A hi-tech look is simple to create and has a very professional feel. Take, for example, the package at left. Glossy black paper looks sophisticatedly festive with the addition of loose-weave silver ribbon. The full bow is deceptively simple to make—just tie three bows, one on top of another, and let the ribbon fall the way it wants to. The silver fronds are not flowers or plant clippings, but floral touches created with glitter sprinkled on glue. They add a delicate feel.

Non-stop parallel lines running over perfect squares make an industrial, yet glittering look. Start by wrapping your package in silver graph-based paper. If the graph is not printed on the bias, cut your piece of wrapping paper at an angle. Select a wide, glossy ribbon, and make three bands around the top half of the package, taping the ribbon snuggly in back so that the three strips are absolutely parallel. Use the graph on the paper as a guide. Next, cut two strips of narrower white ribbon and carefully weave them over and under the silver bands slightly off center of the package; tape them in back. Cut a length of narrow gold ribbon, and place it between the white ribbons, weaving over the silver where the white goes under. If you have taped the ribbon tightly

enough, the weaving will hold every thing in place. You should not have to spoil the clean lines by taping the ribbon in place on the front of the package.

Sometimes it is better to let the gift's own elegance shine through. All this sleek black champagne bottle needs is cellophane to enhance its classic lines. Use a large sheet of cellophane to form a fan behind the bottle. Trim the excess from the front, leaving enough to be caught and secured at the neck by a ribbon. But first, add an exciting touch with gold beads speared on wire with silver tips. Cut the wires long enough so the ends can be wrapped around the bottle neck. Send the gold spears shooting in all directions. Crown this with a ribbon waterfall down the bottle front. Cut several pieces of ribbon, and lay them against the bottle vertically with their middles at the neck. Secure them with another piece of the same ribbon (which also covers up the wire ends), and let the vertical ribbons flop over and down the bottle in a ribbon cascade.

Hi-tech does not always mean metallic. Cover a box with glossy white paper. Use sequin edging, bought in a hobby store, instead of ribbons, making two big loops to put around the box. Next, make two small loops, glue each in a circle, then stick them together.

Apply more glue at the point where the two box bands cross, and press the two small rolls down on the cross at an angle. Finish by dotting little stickers on the box top like confetti.

Contrast black, silver, and gold, then break the symmetry with a shaggy golden bow. Wrap a package with a paper that has a small, tight print. Make two loops with a foil-type gold ribbon, and slip them over the box lengthwise and widthwise. (It is better to use loops rather than one long ribbon so that the gift will lie flat.) Cut six or eight varying lengths of the same ribbon. With another piece of the same ribbon, tie the strips together at their center, then to the crossing point on the gift. Pull the knot as tightly as possible without breaking the ribbon. With your hand, crunch up the tendrils in a haphazard way; just be careful to conceal the central knot with a scrunch or two.

Christmas Wrappings

Minute Christmas tree ornaments make this wrap fun; the little satin cluster is almost bigger than the present! This is a perfect way to make sure a small gift does not get overlooked in the Christmas shuffle. Begin by making a small hole in the top of

the box in which you will wrap your gift. on this gift, wrap the top to the box separately from the bottom. Cut a piece of paper slightly larger than the box top plus its depth. Fold two parallel sides of the paper up and over the sides of the top, and tape the paper down inside. Fold in the obtruding corners of the other sides as you would on any wrap, and tape them inside the box. Do the same procedure on the bottom, making sure you position the box on the paper so the stripes line up when top is on. Clip ten slightly uneven lengths of floral wire. Square them together on one end, and cover the clump of ends with floral tape. Push a small satin ball on the end of each of the pieces of wire. Spread the clump out in a lovely bouquet, then stick the taped end through the hole in the box. Tape it securely on the inside of the top. Save this adornment to use again and again.

Christmas Wrappings

If your gift is romantic, put a little romance in your wrap, too. Use pink and gold wrapping paper and white or gold lacy ribbon to make a large floppy bow. Do not be afraid to experiment with unusual furbelows and fabrics, such as lace, tulle, boas, and velvet. Even a strand of pearls or crystals will communicate the love and excitement of your gift.

A glossy pink paper tells a sweet story that lace or tulle will embellish to

a tee. Choose tulle of a reddish tint and use it almost as you would a ribbon. Cut two pieces and loop one length-wise, the other widthwise, ending on top instead of underneath. Hold the ends in place on top of the gift by tacking a few stitches where they all over-lap. Fan the tulle slightly at the box edges to give a translucent look. Make a light pink tulle bouquet by scrunch-ing a double piece in the middle. Wrap thread around the

underneath center of the bouquet to hold it in place. Attach it to the overlap on the package by taking several stitches. Fluff the bouquet.

A textured
gold paper
with an
extra-long
strand of
pearls is a classic
look, yet also not at all
what one would expect from
a gift wrapping. Buy a long strand
of pearls in a five-and-dime store,
then—very carefully!—snip it.
Take two or three pearls off each end
and knot the string as close to the last
pearls as you can. Wrap the strand
around the package in both directions
as if it were a ribbon. Knot the strands,
then loop them several times around
the knot. Twine the two pearly tails
around the lengthwise strands on the
package. This is a crafty way to dis-
guise a gift of real pearls, with pearl
earrings inside the box. Instead of snip-
ping the strand, however, just unclasp it.

Create luxury and romance with a white boa around pink paper. This wrap is easy to do, but it suggests opulence far beyond its simplicity. Wrap a box in pink paper, then use a feather boa as if it were ribbon. For the cleanest look, make a small knot on the underside of the present, rather than on the top. Less is more in this case.

Use gauzy silver ribbon to extravagant effect against matt white paper. This wrap is almost all ribbon, which works well since the silver has such a rich, yet soft texture. Wrap the ribbon around the gift and, without including the underlying ribbon, tie a knot—not a bow—and leave the ends free. Tie a large, floppy bow over the knot with a fresh piece of ribbon and *voilà* elegance with ease.

Decorate a gold paper with a contrasting silver bouquet made from leaves, cones, and berries. Collect your favorite clippings of holly, mistletoe, and leaves and arrange a small bouquet, tying the pieces together with wire or thread. Gently spray paint the result and let it dry; the paint will make the arrangement hard, and thus easier to handle and longer lasting. If you want contrasting colors in the bouquet, spray paint the components—some white and some silver—before you put the bouquet together. Use thin silver and gold rope twisted together to continue your theme of contrasts. Knot the looping ropes and cut them very close to where they cross. Attach the bouquet with thread or wire to the cross, and you have a look that combines nature with glitter in the most sophisticated way.

Wrap a present in black paper and then soften the stark lines with tulle. Start with a basic wrap done with glossy black paper. Sit the package on a rectangle of tulle (which you can get

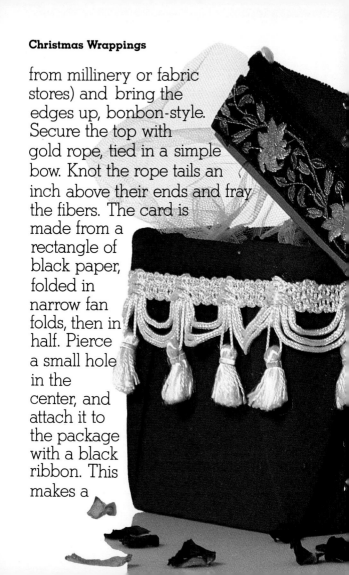

from millinery or fabric stores) and bring the edges up, bonbon-style. Secure the top with gold rope, tied in a simple bow. Knot the rope tails an inch above their ends and fray the fibers. The card is made from a rectangle of black paper, folded in narrow fan folds, then in half. Pierce a small hole in the center, and attach it to the package with a black ribbon. This makes a tiny fan, perfect for writing a name on. This little velvet box is an Aladdin's Cave for small gifts. Take a box and cover the bottom and top separately with burgundy velvet. Let the corner folds show and add texture to the wrap. Glue tasseled trim around the rim of the box bottom, and patterned gold brocade ribbon around the lid. Stick a velvet top knot with a tassel attached on the top of the box. Line the inside of the box with tulle.

Christmas Wrappings

Country wraps suggest freshness and nature. Tissue paper with a small Christmas tree print, like a calico, has a soft, pure air to it, while gingham suggests warm farm kitchens. Cloth ribbon adds a homey texture; if you use red-and-white gingham paper, try using red-and-white gingham cloth ribbon tied in a simple bow—the effect is surprising.

Country wraps look best with natural trimmings. Sprigs of mistletoe or holly; pine cones and tiny tree cuttings add a touch of the out- doors.

Christmas Wrappings

Add small loops of popcorn and cranberries to a plain ribbon instead of a bow.
Paint some small twigs white and mix
them with dried flowers, then twine a
string of cranberries around the whole
thing. Take a walk outside and see what
you find; almost anything will crown a
country wrap.

Tartan ribbon against shiny red
paper combines a little glitter with a lot
of country. The simple bow picks up

the idea of hominess, and the tiny cluster in the center of the bow completes the theme. If you can find a cluster of real berries, that is wonderful. Attach it to the center of the bow with a small piece of wire. You can also obtain fake berries, which can be reused for Christmases to come, at any hobby store.

Add a cozy, warm touch with a home-made nametag. In this case, a small red tin heart has the recipient's name written across its middle. You can do this with paint and a very delicate brush or a glitter pen. Suspended from a floppy, gingham bow, the heart says everything.

One of the easiest ways to wrap an oddly shaped present is in a bag, but be careful to avoid that "oops, I forgot to wrap it" look. One of the easiest methods is to adorn it with a country look of sprigs of cones and cranberries. Wrap a piece of floral wire around the bottom of many tiny pinecones. Wrap several cones into a cluster by twisting their wires, then embellish the cluster with fake holly berries already attached to wires. Alternate the berries and the cones in any combination you choose. Attach the clusters to the top and handles of a shopping bag overflowing with different-colored tissue papers. Take the time to make a few strings of cones and cranberries, and use them for emergencies. Or, as on the red bag at left, cut a country scene of simple shapes out of paper or felt, and glue it right on the bag. The smoke rising from the chimney will bring Christmas cheer.

Red paper patterned with small white flowers is the perfect background for a real twig heart. Take a country walk or a stroll through the park, and pick up as many slender twigs as you can. When you get home, trim them down to a uniform length, about twenty inches (fifty centimeters). Carefully *break* the bunch at the center. Bend each clump into a half heart shape, and wire it in several places onto a wire heart bent from a coathanger. Overlap the two halves in a "v" at the top. Intertwine the twigs at the bottom of the heart. Tie a piece of ribbon at the top, just above the "v." Loop another piece through the first; this will eventually lead to the back of your gift. Before you put the heart on the package, however, get out a black marker and touch up the ends of the twigs. White ends will spoil your clean look.

Make your own country look with

stencils and ribbons—the result is fresh and original. Begin with a box wrapped in white paper; do not use glossy or the ink will not absorb. Buy or make stencils, and arrange them on the box top in an orderly, but slightly random pattern. Sponge over them with different-colored inks. You can also add confetti dots for a new texture. This particular design was inspired by an American patchwork motif; you can find many traditional designs to copy in a visit to the art section of the library. Section the paper with narrow satin ribbon wrapped around the box to accent your pattern. Here, eight separate pieces of ribbon were taped to the inside of the top of the box. This way your creation will not be destroyed when the gift is opened. Run a piece of ribbon along each edge and across the corners of the box. Cross the bottom ribbons in the middle to reflect the heart shape motif.

Christmas Wrappings

Wrapping presents for children provides an excitement all its own. It is hard not to feel some of the anticipation that you felt when you were small, staring hungrily at the delicious presents under the tree. There is no reason why you should not indulge yourself once

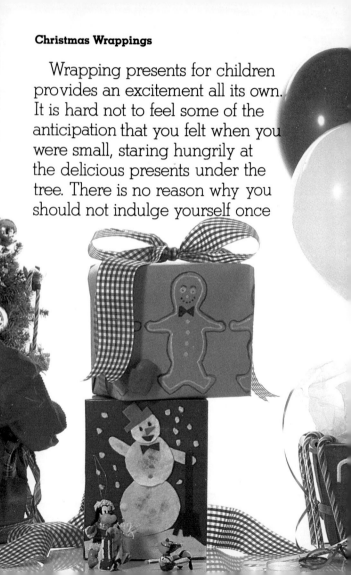

again. Everyone is a child at heart, so
wrap some of your presents
for grown- ups with the
spirit of childhood.
With children's

wrappings—whether for young ones or adults—let your imagination do the work for you. The more intricate a child's wrapping, the better!

In Britain, many children do not hang up Christmas stockings; they put pillowcases at the ends of their beds. Imitate this tradition with a large felt bag—you will be amazed how easily you can fit a large toy in it. Round out the bag by balling up tissue paper for padding, then top it off with a bright bow. Dangle two silver Christmas balls or bells with ribbon, and you have a bag full of possibilities.

Here is a chance to use your best cut-and-paste skills. Wrap the present in glossy red paper. Using squares of white, red, green, orange, and brown felt, cut out a jolly snowman and glue him on your wrap. Do not forget the snow he sits on, the broom he is holding, his jaunty green hat, or his carrot

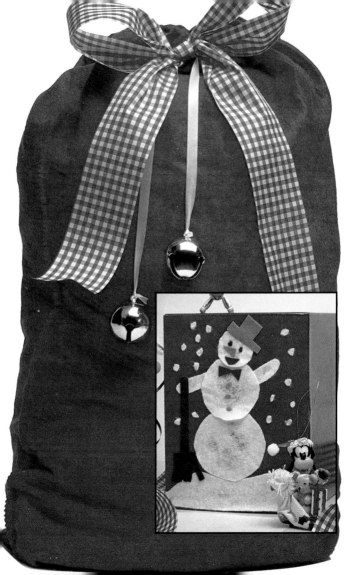

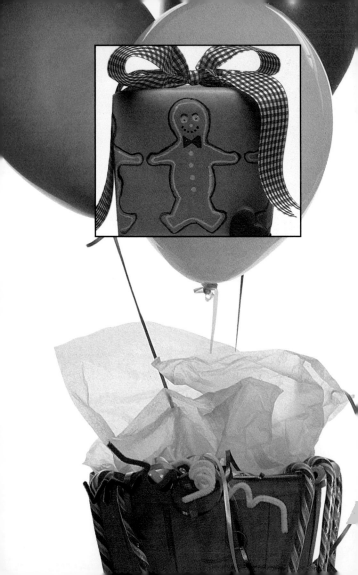

nose. Cut up the white scraps and glue them on as snowflakes. This wrap will pack particularly well for the mail, since all of its sides are flat.

Patterned paper doesn't always have to be purchased. In this case, brown postal paper was laid flat, and gingerbread men were outlined over and over. First thing, measure and cut the exact size of the piece of paper you will use, so you can be sure your gingerbread men will be dancing perfectly. Use a large cookie cutter to trace your outlines, then repeat the shape inside the first outline with a white crayon. In different colors, provide your gingerbread men with buttons, bowtie, and a face. Make a bow with gingham ribbon, but only tie it around two sides of the box so everyone can see your handiwork. As a finishing touch, stick a cookie on the front. There is something edible about your wrap after all!

Christmas Wrappings

Any child will agree that one present is fine, but lots of presents is even better! Find a half-barrel-shaped red basket. Buy three helium-filled balloons and knot them securely to the bottom of the basket. Put all kinds of different things, individually wrapped in colorful tissue paper, into the basket around the balloon strings. Scrunch up a sheet of tissue paper and put it on top so the gifts are hidden. Adorn the barrel edges with candy canes. Now you have a present that's just too good to open!

Combine two boxes and add some fun. This truck is two separate boxes— a shoe box and a flap-lid box. Cover the smaller box (or cab) with red paper and tape it down. Cover both sides of the lid but leave it free to open and close. Cover the shoe box in the same way with white paper. Use labels to make the cab windows and small yellow circle stickers for headlights and red ones for taillights. Make the driver out of one blue sticker and half of a green one. Attach the boxes to one another with brass fasteners, pushed through the box walls from the inside. For wheels, use plastic coffee cup tops fastened to the boxes with thumbtacks through their centers. Tie with a big, red bow.

Christmas Wrappings

How often have you vetoed the perfect gift for someone on your list because you could not figure out how to wrap it? Some basic hints and techniques and a little imagination are all you need to wrap any present—whether over-sized, angular, or oddly proportioned. One strategy is to forget about concealing the gift with your wrapping; it can be intriguingly

enhanced by just gathering cellophane around it and tying it with a bow. Another technique is to put the gift in something larger and more uniform, such as a crate. Be imaginative about camouflaging the crate. Some other suggestions are offered below, but no matter what the gift or the odd-sized problem is, take a good long look and something whimsical and fun is sure to come to you.

Tie a number of small packages for

one person together with the same ribbon to form one present. Stack the boxes on top of each other to form a step pyramid. Using different-colored lengths of curling ribbon to coordinate with the papers on the boxes helps pull the look together. Do not curl each of the tendrils; varying shapes and lengths add a lighthearted air to your gift.

Wrapping cellophane around a present that is already wrapped is an intriguing touch. In this case, the rough corners of an awkwardly shaped gift are muffled in glitter-sprinkled tissue paper. Then the whole thing is smoothed out with an added layer of cellophane. Sit the tissue-surrounded gift in the center of a sheet of cellophane. Bring the corners and edges of the cellophane up over the top of the package, and scrunch them all together to make a close-fitting sack. Tie the sack with several different ribbons for an unexpected look—in this case, wide green, narrow red, and white curling ribbon. Make simple bows, since the ribbons carry a colorful statement. The finishing touch is provided by silver pipecleaners that are slightly twisted.

Fresh-baked gingerbread men are delicious—and when they cluster together in their own basket, they are irresistible! These happy fellows are nestling in a puffy bed of styrofoam packing pieces. Perhaps they are guarding another little present nestled between them. Since these baked goods need to be protected from being eaten too soon, a cellophane sack gathered at the top of the basket handle is a must. Hold the cellophane in place with a tumble of ribbon curls. This hard-to-wrap technique will work with just about any basket or crate. You can find a wide variety of baskets at most household supply

Christmas Wrappings

stores, or you can even recycle crates
for really large gifts.

Combine different stripes on large
presents to keep the eye guessing. Or, if
you run out of paper, improvise with
unexpected paper mixes and hide the
seams with ribbons that
continue your

theme. Make a simple flat bow and tape it on the package a little off center. This is an easy variation on the arcing bow using three even ribbon loops. Flatten the loops and put them on top of each other, spread apart at different angles. Cut a fourth length of ribbon half as long as the others. Fold it in half and cut triangles out of the two ends. Slide this under the three stacked loops. Pull the look together with a cluster of cranberries, strung on thread that also stitches the bow together. Your gift now has a center of focus—who said you were just using scraps?

Personal Designs

Often you want to create a completely individual look with your wrap to tell the recipient that this present is for him or her alone. Tantalize that same person by covering the gift with hints of its contents. Personal designs are great fun because they are so special and tailormade. Later, you may hear some one say, "I remember when all I did was go to movies, and you gave me a present with paper made of movie star post-cards—I do not remember what the present was, but boy, I remember the paper!"

The wonderful thing about a present for a cook is that the trimmings can be as useful in the kitchen as the present itself. Here, wooden utensils accent a classic white-with-pink stripes wrap that is actually a table cloth. Another advantage of using trimmings and wraps like these is that the irregularities of an oddly shaped package are nicely hidden. The ribbon, because of the gift shape, serves mainly to hold the top of the wrap in place. Curling ribbon drapes over the front, and from one front trails a heart cookie cutter. Experiment with the trimmings. Think of clever ways to suggest the present in your wrapping.

This present for the gardener is all trimming; the green tissue paper wrap only serves as a backdrop for the gift. Start with a small earthen vase and stuff it with anything and everything that would appeal to a gardener. This gift

has scissors, a trowel, seeds, and flowers, to name just a few items. Wrap cellophane over the top to hold everything in place and keep inquisitive fingers at bay. The small pink bow anchors the cellophane around the vase, and also contrasts with the green of the paper. Attach a cluster of silk flowers underneath the bow.

If there is someone on your list who is addicted to travel or just an armchair traveller, use a map as wrap. Remember the magnifying glass so the recipient can examine the minutiae of where he or she may go. If places on the map have associations, do not hesitate to mark them. Was someone born in Florence? Or did two people meet in France? Think of more unusual points of interest of trivial facts: mark Elba, where Napoleon spent his last days, or put an asterisk on London and note that Elvis Presley stopped there on March 2, 1960—the only time he set foot in the United Kingdom. With this wrap, be sure the ribbon does not interfere with your handiwork. For your tag, create an imaginary plane ticket with the recipient's name as the passenger.

Lovely marble paper is a luxurious wrapping all by itself. It is particularly appropriate for wrapping books for the reader, since it brings back the days of leather covers and marble end papers, and loving craftsmanship. Buy the paper at a good art supply shop, and use ribbon that accents the marbling. In this case, white and green flat, glossy ribbons gently twisted together and simply knotted add to the understated look. A small rectangle of contrasting marbled paper folded in half serves as an elegant label. For an extra special touch, cover the endpapers of the book with marble paper as well— before you wrap it, of course.

What better than green paper for the sportsperson who spends all of his or her time on the golf course? Use plain white narrow ribbon and make a twist bow. Get a set of shoelaces and tie different-colored golf tees into them, then wind them around the central ribbon knot. Buy colored golf balls and stick them strategically on the paper, gifts in themselves. Make little triangular flags with numbers of the holes on them and stick them on toothpicks. Glue cranberries on top of the green tees like festive and amusing balls.

A Supply &
Shopping List

Here is a checklist that makes over-looking a wrapping essential just about impossible.

- ☐ flat ribbon in several colors and patterns

- ☐ transparent tape

- ☐ scissors

- ☐ white, green, red, and printed tissue paper

- ☐ paper with Santas or snowmen

- ☐ curling ribbon in several colors

- ☐ floral-patterned paper

- ☐ last year's Christmas and Valentine's cards

- ☐ small Christmas ornaments

- ☐ lace; doilies; netting

- ☐ chotchkees and charms

- ☐ mistletoe, holly; pine cuttings

- ☐ glossy red paper

- ☐ any and all of your ideas—plus your imagination!